Cloister

of

My Heart

A Do It Yourself Retreat for Those Seeking Solitude of the Heart in Prayer

ISBN 978-0-9975864-4-2

Unless otherwise stated, all Scripture quotations are taken from the King James Version (KJV) of the Bible.

TABLE OF CONTENTS

Introduction

Heaven on earth. A presence so peaceful. A presence of refuge and rest. A place you never want to leave. This is the secret place of the cloister.

A "cloister" is a covered walk with a wall on one side and a colonnade on the other, usually leading to an enclosed area. I see the cloister as a pathway into the presence of God.

You don't need to go into a deep hidden valley or high up on a mountain somewhere to enter a cloister. Jesus taught us that the heart is a place like a cloister where the King resides. He said, "But thou, when thou prayest, enter into thy closet, and when thou hast shut thy door, pray to thy Father which is in secret, and thy Father which seeth in secret shall reward thee openly" (Matthew 6:6).

What did Jesus mean when He said, "When you pray, enter into your closet"? The word "cloister" also means enclosure. A typical cloister is a quadrilateral enclosure that shelters one in a secret place of prayer. The word "closet" in the Greek language in the first century refers to a typical home in the Middle East with a secret chamber on the first floor. Jesus is telling us to enter into that chamber within our hearts and shut the door. This means that there must be a time every day that we shut out the distractions and enter into our hearts in prayer where He awaits our fellowship. He longs for this fellowship with us more than we long for it ourselves, because indeed we could never love Him as much as He loves us.

Just as a cloister is a quadrilateral enclosure, the Garden of Eden, the Tabernacle of Moses, and the courts in Solomon's Temple were similarly designed with the same pattern. These were the places in the Bible that were designed to be the "habitation of heaven" on earth.

In this book, you will find easy-to-use tools that will help you enter into the secret place of the Most High (Psalm 91:1). This book will also help develop your interior conscience skills based on self-scrutiny. This book is designed that you may fall more in love with the King who resides within your heart. You will be able to enter into and develop a new lifestyle that will help you manage the stress, heartaches, and disappointments that can be so difficult to cope with. I want you to learn how to listen to His voice in order to hear the great and mighty destiny that He has prepared for you.

If there is a heavenly appointment arranged by Divine Providence for you coming up, I want you to be equipped and expecting those miraculous moments with destiny that will change your lives forever.

Beloved, this can only happen through receiving the daily word and inspiration by the Spirit that is available to you in solitude alone with Him. I pray that this "do it yourself" retreat will begin to form within you a new hope. I pray that it will help you hear and stretch your aspirations into a walk that will enable you to possess every word that He has for you. Lastly, I pray that this book will be the gateway into a new intimate relationship with Him that will make you become like Him in everything.

Sincerely,

Dr. Michelle Corral+

Section One

SUPERNATURAL SOLITUDE

John 6:15 KJV
When Jesus therefore perceived that they would come and take him by force, to make him a king, he departed again into a mountain himself alone.

Many of us confuse the excruciating and painful experience of being lonely with being alone. Loneliness is a very painful and heart wrenching social disease. It denotes living abandoned, unwanted, or unloved. Being *alone*, however, is not the same thing as being *lonely*.

Throughout the gospels, each of the writers goes out of their way to insert this unique and unusual lifestyle of solitude and prayer unknown to most rabbis of the first century. In first century Palestine, most rabbis experienced prayer from their daily obedient and reverent devotions around the synagogue. Jesus, as a true "kadosh" or holy rabbi, also remained extremely reverent and observant of this rabbinic tradition by attending synagogue three times a day, as well as participating in the daily prayers, readings, and teachings. He reverenced the formal prayers such as the Amidah prayer (the daily prayer said while standing in the synagogue, now known as the *Shemoneh Esrei*), which He structured the "Our Father" prayer after. Of course, the most important and kadosh of all prayers to an observant first century Jew was the Shema, which was recited twice a day.

Matthew 22:35-38 KJV
[35] Then one of them, which was a lawyer, asked him a question, tempting him, and saying, [36] Master, which is the great commandment in the law? [37] Jesus said unto him, Thou shalt love the Lord thy God with all thy heart,

and with all thy soul, and with all thy mind. [38] This is the first and great commandment.

Also, in addition to the required prayers of the Shema and those of the synagogue, the writers of the gospels spotlight an additional element to Jesus' lifestyle of prayer that was not practiced by the rabbis. This additional element was NOT the norm of rabbinic life. It was an added element, besides life in the synagogue to which He was impeccably observant and reverent.

In order to understand how all four authors of the gospel bring to us this unique identity of solitude, aloneness, and purity of prayer, let us first see Jesus' observance of synagogue life. Historically speaking, it is critical that we perceive Jesus in His historic context. If we do not, then we will have a case of "mistaken identity." Without placing Jesus in His proper Biblical and historical context, we mutilate Scripture and we miss the intent of the gospel and its beauty. My purpose in showing you His life in the synagogue is twofold.

First, we don't want a case of "mistaken identity." We must understand that Jesus was not a renegade, but He was very radical. There is a difference between being a *renegade* and being *radical*. In order to fulfill the criteria of being the Messiah of Israel, the Messiah must be One who keeps the Torah impeccably, but also "builds a fence" around the commandments. He also leads Israel back to Torah by repairing the breaches in its observance. Therefore, we must understand that the gospel clearly teaches us about Jesus' life as an observant rabbi, who reverenced synagogue worship, teaching, and daily prayers.

Luke 4:16 KJV
And he came to Nazareth, where he had been brought up: and, as his custom was, he went into the synagogue on the sabbath day, and stood up for to read.

We see that Jesus went into the synagogue "as was His custom." Luke goes out of his way to tell us this was the daily routine of Jesus as an observant Jew.

Mark 6:2a KJV
And when the sabbath day was come, he began to teach in the synagogue.

John 6:59 KJV

These things said he in the synagogue, as he taught in Capernaum.

Matthew 9:23-26 KJV

[23] And when Jesus came into the ruler's house, and saw the minstrels and the people making a noise, [24] He said unto them, Give place: for the maid is not dead, but sleepeth. And they laughed him to scorn. [25] But when the people were put forth, he went in, and took her by the hand, and the maid arose. [26] And the fame hereof went abroad into all that land.

The writers of the gospels indeed want us to know that Jesus, as the Rabbi of rabbis, observed and cherished the life and prayers of the synagogue.

However, in addition to all of these prayers, observances, and readings, the writers of the gospels show us that Jesus went into a place that no rabbi had

Note:

Jesus' choice to heal on the Sabbath is a demonstration of the reverence and the true rabbinic tradition of Hillel. The purpose of the Sabbath is to give life to man. This was a hotly debated issue between Pharisees from the House of Hillel and the Pharisees from the House of Shammai.

ever gone before. It is a place of solitude prayer. It is patterned after Moses on the Mount alone for 40 days and 40 nights. It is also patterned after Elijah, who went 40 days into aloneness with God on Mount Horeb (1 Kings 19:8).

In reading these texts we must understand that following Jesus into the *secret place* means, "I imitate Christ in His life of prayer." This means that if we are His "talmidim" (the Hebrew word for disciples), then we must follow the Rabbi into an imitation of His life of prayer. Let us see how we can imitate Christ in His life of prayer and solitude. We will also see the miraculous effects of this solitude.

Matthew 14:13 KJV
When Jesus heard of it, he departed thence by ship into a desert place apart: and when the people had heard thereof, they followed him on foot out of the cities.

Mark 1:35 KJV
And in the morning, rising up a great while before day, he went out, and departed into a solitary place, and there prayed.

The "solitary place" that Jesus went to is not just a geographical location void of people; instead, the phrase means "spiritual solitude," which was the result of spending time alone with God in prayer. A solitary place is a condition of the heart that desires nothing in its core but God alone. As we see in Psalm 23:1, "The Lord is my Shepherd; I shall not want." A solitary place is a result of prayer that causes the inward man to be so in love with Jesus that He becomes everything to us. He becomes the sole desire of our heart. Spiritual solitude is this condition of the heart, not just a place apart or alone, although that is also important. If we continue in this context, we will see a second important benefit of going out into a solitary place (solitude of the heart) like Jesus. Let us revisit Mark 1:35.

Mark 1:35 KJV
And in the morning, rising up a great while before day, he went out, and departed into a solitary place, and there prayed.

The writer Mark is telling us that it was still dark. "Rising up a great while before day" means that when it was still dark, Jesus rose up. This is one of the supernatural secrets of the effect of prayer: no matter how dark it is, prayer will always cause you to rise in the darkness. No matter what challenges, hurt, despair, or dilemma that you may be facing, if you will embrace prayer like Jesus did, you will rise. Prayer produces elevation in tribulation.

Beloved, I want to say that it is possible for *every* Christian to follow Jesus into His life of solitude, which in turn will produce spiritual solitude in us. The life of solitude can take place in your chair, at the beach in a secluded secret place of prayer listening to the waves crashing on the shore, or in any place you have set aside for prayer. Entering into spiritual solitude is the first stage of entering into the *Cloister of the Heart.*

There is a difference between silence and solitude. Silence is only the absence of noise. Solitude is a condition of the heart that causes dependence on God for everything. It is how Jesus Christ becomes your all in all, as Kathryn Kuhlman taught us. Solitude detaches the inward man from unreal dependencies that never fulfill or quench the thirst.

Prayer

Lord Jesus,

Take me into Your lifestyle of spiritual solitude. I want to follow You in my life of prayer by entering into the Cloister of My Heart where You reside. Tell me who I am in You and show me who You are.

Section One

Diary
for
Destiny

1. *How can I open up my heart and my life to a lifestyle of solitude with God?*

2. *What are some beginning steps that I can take to enter into a greater life of solitude with the Lord?*

3. *What time in my day can I set apart to devote to God to sit in His presence and spend time with Him?*

4. *Is there a place that I can retreat to and unburden my heart before God?*

5. *Do I consider prayer and devotional time alone with the Lord to be the most important part of my life?*

6. *Is prayer just another thing on my "to do" list? Have I reduced my prayer life to works? If so, how?*

7. *Am I bringing my heart before the Lord every day? Is my heart in a condition of solitude?*

8. *Am I completely and totally dependent on Jesus that I go to Him everyday with everything?*

9. *How can my soul be quenched in the river of God everyday as I come to Him in the secret place? Am I thirsting for this type of communion with God?*

10. *What did I learn about Jesus and His prayer life that I did not know before? Am I willing to follow Him into the solitude?*

11. *Am I solitary in my love for Him?*

My Love Letter to Jesus

Dear Jesus,

Section Two

The Interior Palace

Almost everyone is fascinated with palaces. Some palaces have secret stairways. Some are built up high, majestically standing near a cliff surrounded by the crashing sea. And others have a drawbridge that extends over a water-filled moat that is used to protect and to fortify the palace from intruders. No matter what unique amenities a palace may possess, the most important aspect is that it is the place where the King resides.

The *"Interior Palace"* when compared in context to the Book of Esther helps us understand how the King dwells in the interior palace of the heart. The Book of Esther can be compared to the interior palace of the heart and our life of prayer hidden in the secret place of the Most High.

The Palace
and
The Place of His Presence

In Esther, the author uses an unusual format that is highly irregular when referring to the palace of King Ahasuerus. **The Palace** and the place of His presence are revealed in the book of Esther through a unique literary device. Every time **"the palace"** is mentioned, it is part of the longer phrase "Shushan the Palace." The term for **"the palace"** used in Esther is not the usual word for the living quarters of a monarch, which is *hekal* in Hebrew (Strong's Hebrew 1964). The word used throughout the book of Esther when referring to the living quarters of the King or **"the palace"** is the term *habirah* (Strong's Hebrew 1002).

Habirah is the term King David specially used in Scripture when referring to the place where the Almighty dwelled. "**The Palace**" or "habirah" is a term used by King David to signify the temple of God. In 1 Chronicles 29:1, the last part of the verse says, "For **The Palace** (habirah) is not for man, but for the Lord God."

1 Chronicles 29:19 KJV
And give unto Solomon my son a perfect heart, to keep thy commandments, thy testimonies, and thy statutes, and to do all these things, and to **build the palace***, for the which I have made provision.*

In a literal sense of Scripture, 1 Chronicles 29:1 and 1 Chronicles 29:19 both allude to the temple of God as "**the palace**." In the book of Esther there is a code that Mordecai, its author, used to refer to the temple. He repeatedly used this code in order to awaken the Jews in the diaspora during the Babylonian Medo-Persian captivity to return to Jerusalem because the days of their captivity were expired.

When understanding the life of Esther, we can compare the concept of Esther *in the palace* to the cloister of the heart. In the days of the Persian kings, any girls who were taken into the harem could never leave the palace. Although Esther was queen, she too had to remain behind the walls of the palace. Her life prophetically prefigures a life of prayer hidden in the interior palace of the heart. To remain in *the interior palace* of prayer, one must understand the sweet communion of the soul with the King, Who lives and resides in *"the palace."*

The Spiritual Stages of the Interior Life

Let us take a look at how the interior life develops. The Book of Esther in Chapters 2-5 present to us three spiritual stages that lead us to the throne of the King in prayer.

SPIRITUAL STAGE 1
~*Interior Purification and Formation*~

The Tabernacle in the wilderness and later the Temple in Jerusalem can be defined as the dwelling place of the Divine Presence on the earth. Both the Tabernacle and the Temple were sacred structures given by vision to Moses and later to King David before his decease. *Exodus 25:40 KJV*

And look that thou make them after their pattern, which was shewed thee in the mount.

1 Chronicles 28:19 KJV
All this, said David, the Lord made me understand in writing by his hand upon me, even all the works of this pattern.

This heavenly pattern shown both to Moses on Mount Sinai and to King David were given to them as a pattern or spiritual similitude of the true tabernacles in heaven. Both the Tabernacle and the Temple were composed of three dimensions:

- The Outer Court
- The Inner Court
- The Holy of Holies

These three courts can be compared to the three stages of the interior life. The Holy of Holies is the place of His Throne. The interior palace of the heart where the king resides is an interior temple or palace. In the Book of Esther, Chapters 2-5, Scripture prophetically patterns Esther's experience in the palace that can be compared to our experience in prayer. She never left the palace.

She was hidden in the palace even as our lives are hidden in Christ in God.

Colossians 3:10 KJV
And have put on the new man, which is renewed in
knowledge after the image of him that created him.

Esther prophetically prefigures how the bride should remain in the place of prayer, hidden within the cloister of our own heart. Immediately, upon entering into the palace gates, Esther was taken to the house of women and brought under the custody of Hegai, the keeper of the women. While in the outer court, Esther entered into a preparation process that would eventually lead her to her coronation as Queen of Persia (Esther 2:8-9). This preparation process that led to her coronation as queen is a spiritual similitude of the three stages of the interior life.

Beloved, these three stages can be compared in concept to the three supernatural stages of grace given to the heart that seeks after God in the place of solitary prayer. Patterned after Jesus' life of supernatural solitude and prayer, the interior life must begin with time alone with God.

Psalm 46:10 KJV
Be still, and know that I am God: I will be exalted among the heathen, I will be exalted in the earth.

Zechariah 2:13 KJV
Be silent, O all flesh, before the Lord: for he is raised up out of his holy habitation.

Esther 2:8 KJV
So it came to pass, when the king's commandment and his decree was heard, and when many maidens were gathered together unto Shushan the palace, to the custody of Hegai, that Esther was brought also unto the king's house, to the custody of Hegai, keeper of the women.

One of the meanings of the word "Hegai" in Hebrew is meditation. It also means groaning or separation. The name Hegai as meditation is like the quiet stillness of Spiritual Stage 1 that comes as a result of seeking God through meditation of His Word. This comes from the solitude and aloneness with God in the secret place where we meditate on the daily verses given to us by the Spirit.

If we do not have that holy time alone in solitude, we will miss all of the things He wants to show us about our destinies. In that supernatural solitude the Holy Spirit, our Divine Keeper, reveals to us scriptures that prepare us for the next step in our lives. Likewise, these daily devotional scriptures that come from the fresh manna from heaven every day warn us of impending danger ahead or prophesy to us the blessings that are awaiting us for that day.

Hegai was a keeper of the women that prepared them for entrance into the king's chambers. Comparably, the Holy Spirit as our Divine Keeper begins this supernatural stage of prayer through meditation in God's Word by giving us His heavenly update of what lies ahead. The Scriptures that the Holy Spirit gives to us during this time of supernatural solitude pertain to our own purification. Here He also speedily gives us the things necessary for our purification so that we do not miss our moment with destiny. He will begin the purifying process through daily meditation of the Word as it begins to cleanse us and deliver us from selfishness, self-centeredness, unhealthy egos, or insecurities that become spiritual anxiety disorders.

Let's take a look at Psalm 119:9-16, and pay particular attention to verses 9, 11, and 15.

Psalm 119:9 KJV
Wherewithal shall a young man cleanse his way? by taking heed thereto according to thy word.

Psalm 119:11 KJV
Thy word have I hid in mine heart, that I might not sin against thee.

Psalm 119:15 KJV
I will meditate in thy precepts, and have respect unto thy ways.

Hegai, whose name in Hebrew means meditation, brings us into a deeper purification as we experience meditation in God's Word.

Psalm 1:2 KJV
But his delight is in the law of the Lord; and in his law doth he meditate day and night.

Psalm 19:14 KJV
Let the words of my mouth, and the meditation of my heart, be acceptable in thy sight, O Lord, my strength, and my redeemer.

Psalm 104:34 KJV
My meditation of him shall be sweet: I will be glad in the Lord.

This is the spiritual stage that will prepare us for our destiny by perfecting our thoughts, motives, intentions, and character traits. In this spiritual stage, Esther was given everything necessary for her purification with such things as belonged to her. There are some things that belong to our destinies that cannot be obtained without receiving them in the solitude of the heart through prayer alone with God.

Esther 2:9a KJV
And the maiden pleased him, and she obtained kindness of him; and he speedily gave her her things for purification, with such things as belonged to her.

In this spiritual stage, God will produce much fruit of Christ-like character in us. In Esther 2, the text teaches how Esther began to be perfected in her character through this preparation process, which equipped her for reaching her destiny. The emphasis in Esther 2:10 and Esther 2:20 is on her obedience to Mordecai. The author's intent is to highlight her obedience, because it is a key component to her destiny. It is one of the reasons Esther was elected and selected as queen for such a time as this.

Can you imagine if Esther's character had not been trained and purified in the small tests of obedience? She would have never been able to fulfill the very thing that saved the entire nation of Israel. The type of obedience that Esther displayed was obedience unto death. This obedience to Mordecai allowed her character to be brought up to the highest level of perfection. She obeyed him perfectly behind closed doors when no one was watching but God.

In Esther 4:5, we are shown that all communication between Esther and Mordecai was done through Hatach, who was one of the chamberlains that the king had appointed to Esther, because she lived inside the palace and could never leave. Remember, this type of obedience Esther displayed began to be purified and perfected while she was in the custody of Hegai, the king's keeper of the women.

Esther 2:10 KJV
Esther had not shewed her people nor her kindred: for Mordecai had charged her that she should not shew it.

This quality of Christ-like character revealed in Esther is a prophetic prefiguring of the Bride of Christ. Her destiny was built upon her impeccable obedience. Her obedience was so perfect that it remained constant and consistent even after she became queen.

Esther 2:20 KJV
Esther had not yet shewed her kindred nor her people; as Mordecai had charged her: for Esther did the commandment of Mordecai, like as when she was brought up with him.

Note that verse 20 repeats what was already stated in verse 10, because Scripture is showing us that even after Esther was crowned queen, she continued to demonstrate this character trait that qualified her for the destiny that could have cost her her life.

Beloved, this is also a prophetic prefiguring of how Christ-like character traits are developed in us by prayer. These can only come through the spiritual stage of solitary prayer and meditation on God's Word. Behold, the obedient One who became obedient unto death.

Philippians 2:5 KJV
[5] Let this mind be in you, which was also in Christ Jesus.

Philippians 2:8 KJV
[8] And being found in fashion as a man, he humbled himself, and became obedient unto death, even the death of the cross.

When commanded by Mordecai to intercede for her people, Esther responded in accordance with Scripture:

Esther 4:16b KJV
And so will I go in unto the king, which is not according to the law: and if I perish, I perish.

Prayer

Lord Jesus,

I want to seek after You. I ask You to grant me the grace to separate myself every day to be alone with You. Let me meditate in the solitude of the heart on the daily words You are giving me. I ask You for the grace to enter into this stage of purification. I ask that whatever needs to be built into my character that is necessary for my destiny would be given to me by grace. I ask that all that belongs to me would be released and given as I enter into this daily commitment of secluded solitude of the heart.

SPIRITUAL STAGE 2
~Consecration~

The second spiritual stage that is produced from the solitude of the heart in the interior palace is consecration. Consecration means that something has been dedicated and separated for a purpose. This spiritual stage dedicates and separates your entire being as the personal possession of the Holy Spirit. Consecration is also the spiritual stage of anointing that immerses us in the favor that empowers us to do the impossible.

Esther 2:12 KJV
Now when every maid's turn was come to go in to king Ahasuerus, after that she had been twelve months, according to the manner of the women, (for so were the days of their purifications accomplished, to wit, six months with oil of myrrh, and six months with sweet odours, and with other things for the purifying of the women).

The intent of the author is to prophetically parallel the anointing on Esther with the same anointing on the king of Israel. These twelve months in oils of myrrh and sweet spices are a comparison in concept with Exodus 30:23-24.

Exodus 30:23-24 KJV
[23] Take thou also unto thee principal spices, of pure myrrh five hundred shekels, and of sweet cinnamon half so much, even two hundred and fifty shekels, and of sweet calamus two hundred and fifty shekels, [24] And of cassia five hundred shekels, after the shekel of the sanctuary, and of oil olive an hin.

The purpose in the properties of this oil described in Exodus 30:23-24 is to make an individual the personal property and possession of the Holy Spirit.

Esther 2:15 KJV
Now when the turn of Esther, the daughter of Abihail the uncle of Mordecai, who had taken her for his daughter, was come to go in unto the king, she required nothing but what Hegai the king's chamberlain, the keeper of the women, appointed. And Esther obtained favour in the sight of all them that looked upon her.

Notice how the above text teaches that "she required nothing but what Hegai the king's chamberlain, the keeper of the women, appointed." "Required nothing" means that everything is given in complete surrender. In this spiritual stage, the will becomes united to Him. It wants only what He wants. It desires only what He desires. It desires nothing but Him and wants only His will. This is where we truly become the complete possession of God.

Exodus 30:25 KJV
And thou shalt make it an oil of holy ointment, an ointment compound after the art of the apothecary: it shall be an holy anointing oil.

Exodus 30:31b KJV
This shall be an holy anointing oil unto me throughout your generations.

This is the spiritual stage that consecrates, dedicates, and separates us completely unto Him. Through this empowerment of the anointing, our desire is only for Him. In this spiritual stage during solitary prayer alone with God, the heart requires nothing yet desires only

Him, just as Esther required nothing except the things appointed by Hegai.

Prayer

Lord Jesus,

Take me into the depths of the anointing. Through this anointing please separate, consecrate, and dedicate all that I am only for You. I want You to possess my entire being. I want nothing but Your will.

SPIRITUAL STAGE 3
~Coronation~

The spiritual stage of coronation comes as a result of the purification and consecration effects from the solitude of the heart through aloneness with God in prayer. Just as Esther was brought to Hegai, purification comes to the heart that seeks after God in solitude with Him. Here everything necessary for our destinies is provided as our character is transformed and developed in prayer. As we surrender in the solitude of the heart, daily deliverances and spiritual sensitivities to God's will are perfected and purified in us through the meditation of His Word.

Just as Esther was brought to the second house of the women (Esther 2:14), so does the heart experience purification in the outer court of the interior palace. Hegai, whose name means meditation in Hebrew, purifies the heart by hiding His Word in it. The heart is purified in motives and thoughts by cleansing through His Word (see Psalm 119).

From the spiritual stage of purification in thoughts and motives that come as a result of the mediation on His Word (Hegai), everything that God has ordained that belongs to us for our destinies in Christ is released. Our character is transformed. The character traits necessary for destiny are freely given as Hegai (who is also a type of the Holy Spirit, the Divine Keeper of our souls) prepares us.

Now, before we go more in depth into the third spiritual stage of coronation, let's quickly review the two previous stages already discussed.

In the first spiritual stage of Interior Purification and Formation, Esther received the necessary character traits essential for her destiny, which was obedience unto death. In this stage we too can receive what is necessary for our destiny (Esther 2:9).

The second spiritual stage of Consecration leads us into the inner court of the interior palace. This is the spiritual stage that comes as a result of aloneness with God in the solitude of the heart. Here we become immersed in the anointing that establishes us for our prophetic purpose and destiny.

During this period, we are prepared and empowered for our destiny. The outcome of this spiritual stage is to only desire what He wants. In this place, a heart that has remained in solitary prayer alone with him requires nothing but Him and only what has been appointed.

Esther 2:15 KJV
Now when the turn of Esther, the daughter of Abihail the uncle of Mordecai, who had taken her for his daughter, was come to go in unto the king, she required nothing but what Hegai the king's chamberlain, the keeper of the women, appointed. And Esther obtained favour in the sight of all them that looked upon her.

"She required nothing" is the effect of prayer in the solitude of the heart that causes the fire of holy desire to increase. Remember that it is in this supernatural place of solitude that the heart yearns and desires for His will and great pleasure.

Lastly, we discovered that the third spiritual stage is Coronation. During Coronation, the royal scepter is extended to us. Coronation takes place in the interior palace of the heart where the king resides. It is the place of being robed in royal apparel. Let's take a look at what the text teaches about this in Esther 5:1-2:

Esther 5:1-2 KJV
[1] Now it came to pass on the third day, that Esther put on her royal apparel, and stood in the inner court of the king's house, over against the king's house: and the king sat upon his royal throne in the royal house, over against the gate of the house. [2] And it was so, when the king saw Esther the queen standing in the court, that she obtained favour in his sight: and the king held out to Esther the golden sceptre that was in his hand. So Esther drew near, and touched the top of the sceptre.

In a Hebraic sense of Scripture, royal apparel alludes to the clothing of character traits in the heart. In Hebrew, the concept of clothing is not just something that covers the body. *Middot*, for instance, is the Hebrew word for character, and is derived from one of the Hebrew words for clothing. The type of clothing received during the Coronation stage is royal clothing; more specifically, it refers to clothing the heart with virtue and with character traits.

Exodus 28:2-3 KJV
[2] And thou shalt make holy garments for Aaron thy brother for glory and for beauty. [3] And thou shalt speak unto all that are wise hearted, whom I have filled with the spirit of wisdom, that they may make Aaron's garments to consecrate him, that he may minister unto me in the priest's office.

Scripture mentions two types of garments that were to be made for the high priest. Let's take it verse-by-verse to better understand what God said to Moses.

Exodus 28:2 KJV
And thou shalt make holy garments for Aaron thy brother for glory and for beauty.

Then the text almost seems to contradict itself as it reads:

Exodus 28:3 KJV
And thou shalt speak unto all that are wise hearted, whom I have filled with the spirit of wisdom, that they may make Aaron's garments to consecrate him, that he may minister unto me in the priest's office.

Beloved, we need to understand that the text clearly conveys that the clothing made by Moses came from the commandments of God and the clothing made by the wise-hearted were the actual physical garments to be worn. If we break it down, we see that the text teaches us in Exodus 28:2-3 that the two types of clothing are: 1) the clothing of the heart (middot or character traits); and 2) the clothing that covers the body.

When the king saw Esther standing in the inner court, she was robed in her royal apparel. This text teaches that it was not the earthly king who saw Esther in beautiful clothing, but it was the Heavenly King who beheld Esther in the garments of selflessness and self-sacrifice. He beheld her humility and obedience unto the death. He beheld her desire and petition for God's will alone; therefore, He stretched out the golden scepter and she obtained grace and favor in His sight (see Esther 2:17).

Favor became an unusual characteristic over Esther's life. It was from that day forward that Esther stepped into her highest predestined purpose. Coronation is the diadem of destiny that comes as a result of one's entire life being orchestrated and coordinated by the power of providence in prayer.

Jesus, as a rabbi, embraced this component of prayer, in addition to participating in the life of the synagogue, which He reverenced. This unique lifestyle of solitude in a place apart during the early morning hours or after a day of ministry was rarely practiced. A group of rabbis from the Galilee in the first century known as the *hasidim* (not to be confused with modern-day Hasidim) were known for their exemplary character, radical Torah observance, emphasis on works of chesed (kindness), and solitude alone with God.

Jesus taught His talmidim (disciples) to pray with this same solitude by entering into the interior cloister of the heart. Jesus said in Matthew 6:5-6:

Matthew 6:5-6 KJV
[5] And when thou prayest, thou shalt not be as the hypocrites are: for they love to pray standing in the synagogues and in the corners of the streets, that they may be seen of men. Verily I say unto you, They have their reward. [6] But thou, when thou prayest, enter into thy closet, and when thou hast shut thy door, pray to thy

Father which is in secret; and thy Father which seeth in secret shall reward thee openly.

In the Greek language, the word used for closet is *tameion* (Strong's Greek 5009). A tameion in the first century was a secret chamber in the house used for privacy. In Matthew 6:5, the concept being conveyed is a secret chamber and solitude. The secret chamber is the heart. It is there where the King speaks. It is in the secret of solitude by listening with the heart that we enter into that place of refuge and rest. Let us follow Him into that solitary place of prayer.

Prayer

Lord Jesus,

I ask you to clothe me with your righteousness. Clothe me with Your Christ-like character traits. I ask You to transform me to be like You. I claim the favor Esther radiated in the sight of all who beheld her. I desire to be pleasing in Your Sight.

SECTION TWO

Diary for Destiny

1. *Have I ever entered into this "interior palace of the heart" as the place where the King dwells and desires to commune with me through prayer? If so, explain in detail that experience. If not, why do I believe that I have not experienced this place of prayer yet?*

2. *Figuratively speaking, are there certain rooms, chambers, corridors, or secret passageways in my own heart that I may be afraid of visiting or entering into? If there are certain areas deep within my soul that I tend to avoid or neglect, why do I this?*

3. *Do I have any negative or limited perceptions of God, myself, others, or certain situations? How does the lack of revelation and understanding prevent me from living and residing in "the palace" and having sweet communion of the soul with Him? Explain.*

4. *Am I holding myself to unrealistic expectations of perfection that cause me to feel unworthy of being in His Presence? Do I feel the need to reach a certain standard before I can possess the ability to experience such an intimate place of prayer? Explain.*

5. *Since few seem to experience certain places in God's presence, how can I help lead and encourage others into entering and being with the Lord in the cloister of the heart? Explain.*

My Love Letter to Jesus

Dear Jesus,

SECTION THREE

THE LOVER TO THE BELOVED: THE DIVINE DRAW

~His Redeeming Love~

Drawn by the depths of His love, the Lord sought us and He bought us with His redeeming love.

Matthew 13:45-46 KJV
[45] Again, the kingdom of heaven is like unto a merchant man, seeking goodly pearls: [46] Who, when he had found

one pearl of great price, went and sold all that he had, and bought it.

Beloved, you are the pearl of great price to the Son of God. He sought after you, and bought you with the *great price* of Calvary's cross.

John 19:28 KJV
After this, Jesus knowing that all things were now accomplished, that the scripture might be fulfilled, saith, I thirst.

The text teaches that Jesus cried out on Calvary's cross the words of His travail, "I thirst." This cry that came forth from the Master defines the depths of the search that saved our souls. They were the words that drove Him to the destiny of the cruel cross of Calvary. These words were the summation of the love that fueled the fire that kept rising after every fall under the weight of that heavy cross. It was His thirst that propelled Him through His Passion. The thirst that Jesus expressed was not for something to drink. The thirst that He conveyed was for fellowship and communion with everyone that would become His own by the price He paid on the cross. This was in fulfillment of Psalm 69:21.

Psalm 69:21 KJV
They gave me also gall for my meat; and in my thirst they
gave me vinegar to drink.

The grace of God and the immeasurable love of Christ are revealed in the words "I thirst." It reveals that He is the One who first thirsts for us. Just as the merchant in Matthew 13 is set on a journey seeking goodly pearls, so has the Son of God set out on a journey to seek your soul. Therefore, we must understand that everything that happens in prayer as the soul is drawn into Him does not happen because we sought Him, but because He seeks us.

The heart that does not understand this divine drawing into Him can become deceived by thinking that we are the ones who are seeking Him, when in reality He is the One who has sought after us. At the Last Supper on the night that He was betrayed, knowing His disciples would defect and default, He assures them with this confidence. He tells them these words to instill confidence; otherwise, condemnation would have tortured them with guilt.

John 15:16a KJV
Ye have not chosen me, but I have chosen you, and ordained you, that ye should go and bring forth fruit, and that your fruit should remain.

Beloved, there is a grace and comfort in knowing that God is aware of our weaknesses, frailties, and imperfections. He comforts us through the assurance of knowing that He is the Lover and we are the Beloved. He has sought after us. He thirsts for us. He has chosen us. And through love He draws us into Himself. We do not bring ourselves to prayer; instead, He brings us, draws us, and woos us as a Lover woos the Beloved.

Song of Solomon 1:4a KJV
Draw me, we will run after thee: the king hath brought me into his chambers.

Song of Solomon 2:4 KJV
He brought me to the banqueting house, and his banner over me was love.

Beloved, not only does He lead us, seek after us, and thirst for us, but He also through grace elevates the heart into heights through a greater revelation of who

He is. The experience of the transfiguration shows us that we have nothing to do with the grace freely given to us. We need only respond to the knocking and bidding of the Beloved as He seeks us.

Let us not resist the bidding of the Lover to the Beloved with such futile excuses that are worthless and profit nothing.

Song of Solomon 5:2-3 KJV
[2] I sleep, but my heart waketh: it is the voice of my beloved that knocketh, saying, Open to me, my sister, my love, my dove, my undefiled: for my head is filled with dew, and my locks with the drops of the night. [3] I have put off my coat; how shall I put it on? I have washed my feet; how shall I defile them?

The excuses of the Beloved are futile as to why she is not opening up her heart. So the Lover seeking her shows us how we so easily forfeit the available grace by not responding to the call to prayer. We too use excuses that are equally as futile as hers:

- "I have to write this paper."
- "I need to watch the news."

- "I prayed yesterday."
- "I don't feel anything when I pray."
- "I don't need anything, so why should I pray?"
- "I never hear God's voice like Sister or Brother So-and-so, so why should I pray?"

But the *worst* excuse of all is, "I sinned, I said something or did something that makes me unworthy to be in His Presence." Beloved, let me tell you why these excuses are futile. They are worthless, petty, and deadly distractions that prevent our souls from the deliverance, the directions, and the depths of healing that He longs to give us.

Let us look at the monumental mistake that Peter made, based on his fear of the cross and his inability to fully follow Jesus until the resurrection. This is recorded in Scripture not so we know that it happened, but so we understand that nothing, absolutely *nothing,* can separate us from the love of God in Christ Jesus (Romans 8:39).

In Matthew 16:22-25, Peter in his flesh begins to rebuke Jesus. Let's take a look at verses 22 and 23:

Matthew 16:22-23 KJV
[22] Then Peter took him, and began to rebuke him, saying, Be it far from thee, Lord: this shall not be unto thee. [23] But he turned, and said unto Peter, Get thee behind me, Satan: thou art an offence unto me: for thou savourest not the things that be of God, but those that be of men.

Beloved, in the context of this miserable mistake, Jesus does something that is recorded in Scripture that changes Peter forever. The Lover knows that the Beloved is already under condemnation over his miserable mistake. The Bible tells us how Jesus is going to draw Peter into a place of His Presence that few will ever experience.

Matthew 17:1-2a KJV
[1] And after six days Jesus taketh Peter, James, and John his brother, and bringeth them up into an high mountain apart, [2] And was transfigured before them.

Beloved, this is an example we cannot possibly conceive of in our hearts, how we could have anything to offer on our own that could merit such an experience like the transfiguration. Jesus took Peter up to the high mountain right after the miserable mistake in Matthew 16:22-23. This shows us that the miserable excuse of condemnation and guilt that says, "I'm not worthy" should never keep us from prayer. Quite the contrary, whenever we make a mistake He is waiting to take us to our transfiguration experience with Him.

Esther, for example, was brought to the palace of the king not of her own accord.

Esther 2:1-2 KJV
[1] After these things, when the wrath of king Ahasuerus was appeased, he remembered Vashti, and what she had done, and what was decreed against her. [2] Then said the king's servants that ministered unto him, Let there be fair young virgins sought for the king.

Just as the king's servants at the king's command sought for a bride, so does the King seek after us, to take us apart into a place to prepare us for the interior palace.

Prayer

Precious Jesus, I give you praise and honor and glory! Help me to always thirst for You and to long for You. Remind me that You are always seeking me. Transform me and transfigure me into the person You have called me to be. Cause me to come up higher in every area of my being. When I make mistakes, help me to quickly repent and to turn to You. In Your blessed name, amen!

SECTION THREE

Diary for Destiny

1. *What are some of the ways in which the Lord has drawn me into the place of His Presence? Am I always sensitive to His callings and drawings?*

2. *Similar to the Beloved in Song of Solomon, have I also been resisting "the bidding of the Lover"? What kind of futile excuses am I making that restrict my soul from receiving blessings that the Lord longs to give me?*

3. *What other challenges, obstacles, or distractions keep me from responding to the Lover of my soul, and therefore, are holding my soul in captivity?*

4. *What are my true motives for seeking the Lord? Are my motives pure? Do I pray only when I am trouble and need to make a request to Him?*

5. If I have I been deceived into thinking that I am the one seeking the Lord (when in reality He is the One seeking after me), how may I better understand this divine drawing to Him?

6. *As I have learned of the thirst that Jesus has expressed for fellowship and communion with me, how may I continually thirst for Him, stop making excuses, and respond without resistance?*

7. *What mistakes have I made in my life that can be compared to the "miserable mistake" that Peter made in Matthew 16:22-23? Did I allow guilt and condemnation to keep me away from my own transfiguration experience that Jesus had waiting for me? What could have been done differently? Explain in detail.*

My Love Letter to Jesus

Dear Jesus,

Section Four

Guarding

The Garden

~Examination of Conscience and Self-Scrutiny~

The term "interior life" can be compared to our interior soul with its emotions, faculties of reason, conscience, and will. It is the inward "palace" where the Lord resides. It is also like a hidden garden.

In Hebrew, one of the words for soul is *neshamah* (Strong's Hebrew 5397). The word *neshamah* in Hebrew is related to two similar words that help us understand its deeper meaning. The first word related to *neshamah* (soul) is "heaven." Heaven translated from English to

Hebrew is the word *shamayim* (Strong's Hebrew 8064). The second term in Hebrew related to the word *neshamah* (soul) is *ha shemen* (Strong's Hebrew 8081), which means "the oil." These two terms *ha shemen* (the oil) and *shamayim* (heaven) give us insight to the hidden meaning of soul.

For example, throughout Scripture the text teaches us that the concept of "soul" can be compared to a "watered garden."

Isaiah 58:11 KJV
And the Lord shall guide thee continually, and satisfy thy soul in drought, and make fat thy bones: and thou shalt be like a watered garden, and like a spring of water, whose waters fail not.

In a literal sense of Scripture, the first ministry that God gave man was the ministry to "guard the garden" (Genesis 2:15). This first ministry can be compared in context to the first priority of every Christian. This is why we must understand how to guard the garden of our interior souls through prayer and examination of conscience. Guarding the garden involves some work on our parts. Just like gardeners in the natural, we must cultivate our thoughts, emotions, will, and faculties through prayer and self-scrutiny.

In Genesis 2:15 the text teaches us, "And the Lord God took the man, and put him into the Garden of Eden to dress it and to keep it." The Hebrew verb for "to dress" used here in Genesis 2:15 is the verb *abad* (Strong's Hebrew 5647). *Abad* is a word with multiple meanings in Hebrew. It is usually used in reference to "labor" or "service" and more specifically used in Scripture to denote "priestly service" and "worship." It is also often used in reference to ministry in the Tabernacle and later to ministry in the Temple. This type of ministry is translated in Hebrew as *avodah* (from Strong's Hebrew 5656). The priests, who served in the Tabernacle and later in the Temple, were called the *avadim* or "servants."

Psalms 134:1 KJV
Behold, bless ye the Lord, all ye servants of the Lord, which by night stand in the house of the Lord.

Psalms 135:1-2 KJV
[1] Praise ye the Lord. Praise ye the name of the Lord; praise him, O ye servants of the Lord. [2] Ye that stand in

the house of the Lord, in the courts of the house of our God.

One of the ways that we interpret the Bible is through developing proper hermeneutical skills. Hermeneutical skills are not just for theologians, but are something we can easily learn and develop to properly make an analysis of the text. For example, if we were to study Genesis 1 and 2, we should not just read these chapters as if we are reading a newspaper. First, we must discover the *intent* of the author. In the case of Genesis 1 and 2, Moses is going out of his way to use the terminology of the Tabernacle when referring to the garden. He shows us in Genesis 2:15 that the *avodah* (service) of Adam was to be a keeper of the Tabernacle of God's presence on earth in the garden.

Moses uses certain "Tabernacle terms" in Genesis 2 for the purpose of defining the first destiny of Adam as a priest. Here we are able to see that Adam was chosen in his *avodah* (service) to cultivate God's presence in the garden. In Genesis 2:5-6, Moses tells us that there was a mist that went up from the earth to water the whole face of the ground because there was not a man to till the ground. In a literal sense of Scripture, the phrase "to till" in English translates to *abad* in Hebrew. The mist going up to water the whole face of the ground hermeneutically implies that the mist is the glory of God. The mist going up and filling the garden parallels the glory of the Lord covering and filling the Tabernacle.

Exodus 40:34 KJV
Then a cloud covered the tent of the congregation, and the glory of the Lord filled the tabernacle.

In Genesis 2:10, the text teaches that there was a river that went forth from the garden into four heads. Once again Moses communicates his intent and purpose by documenting the details in the garden that correspond with the Tabernacle so that we will understand man's greatest ministry and destiny. The implementation of these "Tabernacle terms" helps us to be able to easily compare these concepts.

Exodus 25:10 KJV
...and you shall make an ark...

Exodus 25:12 KJV
And you shall cast four rings of gold for it...

Exodus 25:23 KJV
And you shall make a table...

Exodus 25:26 KJV
And you shall make for it four rings of gold, and put the rings in the four corners that are on the four feet thereof.

In Exodus, Moses presents the prophetic patterns of the Tabernacle given to him on the mount in "fours."

Exodus 25:40 KJV
And look that thou make them after their pattern, which was shewed thee in the mount.

Exodus 25:8b KJV
...As it was shewed thee in the mount, so shall they make it.

In Exodus 27:1-2 and Exodus 27:4, the concept of "four" is accentuated and elaborated to compare in context the river with four heads that came out of the garden in Eden. The text teaches:

Exodus 27:1-2, 4 KJV
[1] And thou shalt make an altar of shittim wood...the altar shall be foursquare: [2] And thou shalt make the horns of it upon the four corners thereof: [4] And thou shalt make...four brasen rings in the four corners thereof.

Verses 11 and 12 in Genesis 2 reveal another correlation between the garden and the Tabernacle.

Genesis 2:11-12 KJV
*[11] ...that is it which compasseth the whole land of Havilah, where there is gold; [12] And the gold of that land is good: there is **bdellium** and **the onyx stone.***

There are two elements in these scriptures that we should pay close attention to. In terms of the Tabernacle, bdellium and the onyx stone are very important. Onyx stones are the stones used exclusively in the breastplate of the high priest. The onyx stone in the breastplate was worn by the high priest of Israel while performing his *avodah* (service) in the Tabernacle. Bdellium is the color of manna. From this we can ascertain that the food given to Adam in the garden was based on the commandments of God and His Word.

Exodus 28:15-20 KJV
[15] And thou shalt make the breastplate of judgment with cunning work; after the work of the ephod thou shalt make it; of gold, of blue, and of purple, and of scarlet, and of fine twined linen, shalt thou make it. [16] Foursquare it shall be being doubled; a span shall be the length thereof, and a span shall be the breadth thereof. [17] And thou shalt set in it settings of stones, even four rows of stones: the first row shall be a sardius, a topaz, and a carbuncle: this shall be the first row. [18] And the second row shall be an emerald, a sapphire, and a diamond. [19] And the third row a ligure, an agate, and an amethyst. [20] And the fourth row a beryl, and an onyx, and a jasper: they shall be set in gold in their inclosings.

Now, let's take a look at Numbers 11:6-7 to see another connection, with verse 7 being our key verse:

Numbers 11:6-7 KJV
[6] But now our soul is dried away: there is nothing at all, beside this manna, before our eyes. [7] And the manna was as coriander seed, and the colour thereof as the colour of bdellium.

We see here that Moses places a comparison in the context by the words used in Genesis 2 to describe the gold, the "fours", the stones, and the bdellium. These components from the garden perfectly parallel the components of the Tabernacle. He connects the components to clarify that the *avodah* (service) of Adam given in the garden is one that called him to guard, protect, and cultivate the presence of God. This ultimately teaches us that man was created in his highest destiny to serve in God's presence.

Self-Scrutiny

Guarding the garden of our soul also involves self-scrutiny and using our conscience and faculties of reason. The conscience is a very important part of our inner man that is created with the faculties of reason. Reasoning skills that empower us to know the difference between good and evil are the most basic of conscience faculties.

Paul says in Romans 2:15 that everyone is created with a conscience "which shew the work of the law (Torah) written in their hearts, their conscience also bearing witness, and their thoughts the mean while accusing or else excusing one another."

The book of Hebrews teaches us that spiritual maturity is developed from conscience skills. The writer of Hebrews explains that the more God's Word is given to us in its true prophetic and applicable meaning, then the more self-scrutiny and conscience skills will be developed.

Hebrews 5:13-14 says, "For every one that useth milk is unskillful in the word of righteousness: for he is a babe. But strong meat belongeth to them that are of full age, even those who by reason of use have their senses exercised to discern both good and evil."

In order to enter into the place of rest and intimacy, God wants us to be able to always be in truth about our issues. Why do we try to cover them up? Why are we so afraid to confront ourselves when He already knows and loves us so unconditionally? We oftentimes use the "fig leaves" of blaming others or making excuses, rather than just giving to God our limitations, frailties, and coping mechanisms that are sometimes damaging to who we are and to others.

Look at Adam. When God cried to Adam, "Adam, where are you?", we see that Adam hid from God because he was afraid (Genesis 3:10). Fear is the source of spiritual anxiety disorders and deception that distort the truth in us. David said, "Thou desirest truth in the inward parts: and in the hidden part thou shalt make me to know wisdom" (Psalm 51:6).

How can we have intimacy with our Father when we hide and cover up our pain, our limitations, our frailties, and our sin from Him? He is Truth, and they that worship Him must worship Him in Spirit and in Truth (John 4:24). Entering into the cloister of the heart is an experience of deliverance deep within us.

Here is how David began his prayer of self-scrutiny: "Search me, O God, and know my heart: try me and know my thoughts" (Psalm 139:23). To David, the search was an important part of his intimate fellowship in the secret place. We can refer to the "search" that David requested of God as an examination of heart and conscience. David says, "Search me" in Psalm 139, and in Psalm 26:2, David requests, "Examine me, O Lord, and prove me; try my reins and my heart." Psalm 26:3 says, "For I have walked in thy truth."

What does it mean to "try the reins and the heart"? The word "reins" is taken from the Hebrew word "kilyah" (Strong's Hebrew 3629) which is the same Hebrew word as kidneys. What does it mean to "try my kidneys"? Trying my kilyah (kidneys) refers to the Biblical concept of self examination that becomes developed by the truth of God's Word and discernment of one's own motives ("kavanah" in Hebrew). Just as the kidneys filter out toxins, so does God desire our inward faculties to filter and process our thoughts and emotions that stir us to actions and deeds. Our thoughts govern our actions. This is why our thoughts need to be corrected and directed under the dominion of the Word and His will. As 2 Corinthians 10:5 says in the last part of the verse, we are to bring "into captivity every thought to the obedience of Christ."

David perceived distorted thoughts and denial of one's true motives as something that hindered his fellowship with God. David said in Psalm 66:18, "If I regard iniquity in my heart, the Lord will not hear me." Let us receive full deliverance and healing, and surrender every secret sorrow and secret fault to the Lord. Let us enter into the Interior Palace with grace and truth. As Psalm 19:12 says, "Who can understand his errors? Cleanse thou me from secret faults."

Self-Scrutiny Examen

Take time daily to answer these questions in your devotional time alone with the Lord.

Particular Examen:

Am I using any "cover ups" in my thoughts to avoid ownership of an attitude or motive?

General Examen:

Has the "cover up" affected my relationship with others based on a distorted view of the truth?

Particular Examen:

Am I afraid to show God my true feelings and motives?

General Examen:

Why am I covering up? Did I forget that the Omniscient One already knows and loves me completely?

Particular Examen:

Do I give God all my secrets?

General Examen:

Am I having a hard time surrendering a particular attitude or thought to the grace of God? Am I trying to do this on my own, or do I see myself as someone completely destitute of my own righteousness, trusting the grace of God to cover me with His righteousness?

- Make a declaration by faith that you will always acknowledge the victories and not be stumbled by the falls. It is your desire that God is seeing. Proverbs 24:16 says, "The righteous fall seven times and riseth up again."

- Write down the areas of fall and the victories that you have received in Christ.

- Write a short essay on why you should not be discouraged over your falls.

- Document details of your personal challenges. Explain how the Lord faithfully delivered you, is changing you, and is working to use this for His glory.

Prayer

Lord Jesus, enter this garden. Cleanse and prune. Cut back every attitude or wicked thought that is based in distorted thinking by not taking ownership. Help me not to hide. I want to show You everything. Give me the grace to trust you to deliver me from the most painful excruciating circumstances of my life. Help me to discern myself and know that I am completely loved by You. Amen!

SECTION FOUR

Diary for Destiny

1. *In what ways can you "till the ground" of your interior soul?*

2. Based on what you have learned, what would you say is your highest destiny, or avodah to God?

3. *What does avodah to God in the garden look like for you?*

4. Guarding the garden of our interior souls involves some work on our parts. What are some practical ways to incorporate prayer and self-scrutiny skills of your neshamah (interior soul) into your daily life?

My Love Letter to Jesus

Dear Jesus,

Chesed Publications

What is Chesed?

Chesed means "loving kindness" in Hebrew. Our publication house is called Chesed Publications because when you purchase a book, you are helping us to do the impossible for people that could never help themselves.

We provide daily feeding programs to orphans and grandmothers, pay for educational fees for children in our orphan homes, conduct medical missions throughout the world, purchase clean water wells, and so much more.

In April 2016, Chesed Publications was founded to financially support Dr. Michelle Corral's vision of acts of chesed to the poor, along with the mission to pass on the wealth of teaching that God entrusted to her to the next generation.

Books Authored by Dr. Michelle Corral

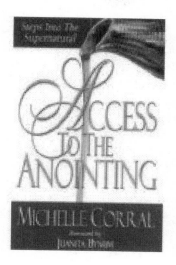

For a Complete List of
CDs and Ministry Resources

Contact:

Breath of the Spirit Prophetic Word Center
P.O. BOX 2676
Orange, CA 92669

Phone # (714) 694-1100

Youtube.com/DrMichelleCorral
Word Network on Mondays
@ 10:30 pm PST
www.breathofthespirit.org
www.drmichellecorral.com
facebook.com/Dr.Corral

Made in the USA
Charleston, SC
24 July 2016